Sailor's Home

Selected Bibiography — (Poetry collections only)

Arjen Duinker
> Ook al is het niet zo
> De geschiedenis van een opsomming
> The Sublime Song of a Maybe (trans. Willem Groenewegen)
> Misschien vier vergelijkingen
> De zon en de wereld: gedichten voor twee stemmen
> The Sun and the World: poems for two voices (trans. jeltje)

W.N. Herbert
> The Testament of the Reverend Thomas Dick
> Forked Tongue
> Cabaret McGonagall
> The Laurelude
> The Big Bumper Book of Troy

Uwe Kolbe
> Hineingeboren. Gedichte 1975-1979
> Abschiede und andere Liebesgedichte
> Bornholm II
> Nicht wirklich platonisch
> Vineta
> Die Farben des Wassers

Peter Laugesen
> Når engle bøvser jazz
> Trashpilot
> Helt alene i hele verden og hip som ind i helvede
> Radio Fiesole; Grassinan Cantos
> Forstad til alt

Karine Martel
> Textures
> Poème pour un marin
> Franchir la peau

Yang Lian
> Yang Lian Zuo Pin 1982 - 1997 (2 volumes)
> Yang Lian Xin Zuo 1998 - 2002
>
> Where the Sea Stands Still (translated by Brian Holton)
> Yi (translated by Mabel Lee)
> Notes of a Blissful Ghost (translated by Brian Holton)
> Concentric Circles (translated by Brian Holton)

A miscellany of poetry by
Arjen Duinker, W.N. Herbert, Uwe Kolbe,
Peter Laugesen, Karine Martel and Yang Lian

with English translations

Curated by Yang Lian

Shearsman Books
Exeter

First published in the United Kingdom in 2005 by
Shearsman Books Ltd
58 Velwell Road
Exeter EX4 4LD

www.shearsman.com

ISBN 0-907562-86-8

Acknowledgements
The authors and the publisher gratefully acknowledge the financial assistance
of Jenny Hall, without which this publication, and the event that occasioned it,
would not have been possible.

W.N. Herbert's poem 'A Midsummer Light's Nighthouse' was previously broad-
cast on BBC Radio 3.

The photograph of Uwe Kolbe is copyright © Marcus Hammerschmitt, 2005;
the photograph of Peter Laugesen is reproduced by courtesy of Borgen Forlag,
Valby, Denmark. The remaining photographs are reproduced here by courtesy
of Jacqueline Koster (Arjen Duinker), Qiu Leilei (Yang Lian), Vincent Hart
(Karine Martel) and Stephanie R Mickler (W. N. Herbert). The front cover
photograph, a detail of which also appears on the title page, was kindly supplied
by Iege Vanwalle.

Contents

Sailor's Home
Festival Programme

1. Opening Party for invited quests —
At the sponsor's home. From 8.00 pm, 21 October, 2005.

2. First Reading —

W.N. Herbert and Yang Lian.
At the sponsor's home. 3.00 pm, 22 October, 2005.

3. Second Reading —

Arjen Duinker and Karine Martel.
At the sponsor's home. 8.00 pm, 22 October, 2005.

4. Third Reading —

Uwe Kolbe and Peter Laugesen.
At the sponsor's home. 3.00 pm, 23 October, 2005.

5. Closing Event — Discussions

How Does the Sailor Find His / Her Way Home ?
Host: Fiona Sampson

Gate Theatre, 11 Pembridge Road, London W11.
From 7.00 pm, 23 October, 2005.

Sailor's Home – A Preface

How long ago is it since poetry became public property? Today, poets write with the idea of publishing in our minds, and poetry books are published with the idea of sales in the publisher's minds (however few!). Even poetry events seem to be organised according to the numbers of tickets that can be sold. The public has become an invisible hand, playing with and controlling the standards of the poetry world, and as such has transformed it into just as dull a field as any other directly commercial endeavour.

This is not the same thing as saying poets have no duty to communicate: we don't want simply to deny a role to the public, but to state a preference for the way people have chosen to interact with poets in every ancient culture for thousands of years — by listening and reading. By leaving the poets alone with the act of creation, to follow our individual, often quite mad, compositional routes.

The power of the public is equal to the power of posterity: it decides which poems, which poets, will survive and continue to be read. But before this selection has been made, as poems are being created, no exterior body should pronounce on poetry, and no one should presume to pronounce on its behalf. No one genuinely knows what 'the public' is, or what it 'wants', and creativity is not an act of second guessing. All a poet can do is to listen to that voice sounding in their inner depths — not even determining whether this is heart, soul or mind, not even defining what these units might be — and then compel language to follow that voice through an intense engagement with craft. We believe the poetry arising from this individual act is more beautiful than any expensive book and more noble than any would-be bestseller.

Since antiquity poets have enaged in dialogue with other poets. When the great Tang Dynasty poets Du Fu and Li Bai met, they did not write for the public, they didn't even know if someone would collect and publish their works after their deaths. They simply wrote to each other, in order to deepen and enjoy the friendship they felt; to give each other solace in difficult, often cruel times. Also (and this is no secret for any poet!) to meet the challenge of responding to an equal talent. The type of composition explored in such exchanges has to be a private act pursued with professional fervour. This unique combination allowed their poetry to reach such a high standard that posterity has acknowledged them: we continue to read them today. We are their public.

Sailor's Home is a private poetry festival being held in London from the 21-23 October, 2005. It is also the title of a body of poems written by six poet-friends in their different languages. We are: Bill Herbert who writes in English (and Scots); Arjen Duinker who writes in Dutch; Uwe Kolbe in German, Peter Laugesan in Danish, Karine Martel in French, and Yang Lian in Chinese.

The poems in this book do not 'respond' to each other in a narrow sense: each poet has explored his or her own understanding of the title 'Sailor's Home', and arrranged their individual forms accordingly. So here there are at least six boats setting sail on different waterways, rivers, lakes – and all seven seas. But who is to say sailors don't catch sight of each other in the distance? The ocean of language beneath our keels forms a deep link between us: by touching its waves, we share the joys and dangers of navigation. We all leave harbour constantly, seeking a new home in each new poem.

As well as the poems in both originals and translations into English, this book contains details of the festival's conception and programmes. It is the document of this unique event. We have tried to bring to the festival the finest thing we could create in each language, in order to exchange it with others in the readings and discussions. The idea of a truly international exchange is not just an empty phrase: it is based on the specific value of these local voices. Six distinctive writers have collaborated to develop our understanding of both human society and of poetry. Crossing time and space like all sea travellers, they show how poetry can carry the freight of that individual inner voice – privately and professionally.

Yang Lian (and W.N. Herbert)
London
August, 2005

Arjen Duinker

with English translations by jeltje

Arjen Duinker was born in Delft in 1956 and continues to live and work there. He has published a novel, *Het Moeras* (The Morass, 1992), and nine volumes of poetry in The Netherlands, all from Meulenhoff Publishers, Amsterdam.

He made his debut as a poet in 1988 with the volume *Rode oever* (Red Shore). In 2001 he received the prestigious Jan Campert prize for his volume *De geschiedenis van een opsomming* (The History of an Enumeration; 2000). His most recent collection *De Zon en de Wereld* (The Sun and the World) won the 2005 VSB Poetry Prize, and has recently been published in English translation in Australia. His work has been translated into several languages and book-length collections have also appeared in France, Portugal, Italy, and the UK, the latter from Arc Publications. Further volumes are in preparation in China, Finland, Iran, Croatia and Mexico. One of his poems was translated into 220 different languages for a project entitled "World Poem". Together with the French poet Karine Martel he has written *And that? Infinite*, which will be published in Amsterdam in 2006.

Sailor's Home

I

De roep van de golven rood.
Een bloem glijdt door een glooiing
En geeft haar parfum aan een steilte
Die vrij in de lucht zwijgt.

De trots van de golven zwart.
De ogen roven het onverwachte
Dat de striemen op de huid
Met blaadjes kalmeert.

Sailor's Home

I

Red, the call of the waves.
A flower slides down a slope,
Gives her perfume to a steepness
Free and silent in the air.

Black, the pride of the waves.
Eyes steal the unforeseen
Appeasing the lashes
On the skin with petals.

2

De wimpers breken het verlangen.
De motoren stampen het verlangen fijn.

Cadans in de lippen, cadans in het bloed!
Wind, jaag het gruis naar alle kanten, wind!

Laat het glinsteren in het donker, nacht zijn overdag!
Cadans in de vingers, cadans in het haar!

De motoren proeven hijgend van de olie.
De wimpers zien de olie in een waaier.

2

The eyelashes break desire.
The motors pound desire to a pulp.

Cadence in the lips, cadence in the blood!
Wind, chase the grime every way, wind!

Let it sparkle in the dark, night become day!
Cadence in the fingers, cadence in the hair!

Panting, the motors taste of the oil.
The eyelashes see oil in a fan.

3

Beukende kammen en gillende snavels . . .
Uiteinden van woorden in dikke walmen . . .
Het schip verdoezelt de wegen door het idioom,
Maakt omgekeerde krassen in de spiegel,
Het hart van de zee groeit aan en aan . . .

Waar de bloem haar schoonheid toont,
Verdampen zoute dauwdruppels in het gefluister
Van vlinder en lucht.

3

Battering combs and shrieking beaks . . .
Extremities of words in clouds of thick smoke . . .
The ship disguises the ways through the idiom,
Scratches in reverse in the mirror,
The heart of the ocean keeps on expanding . . .

Where the flower shows her beauty
Salty drops of dew evaporate in whispers
Of butterfly and sky.

4

Siddering met staart
Op de rug, ogen
Zien twee lippen.

Waar de bloem haar schoonheid toont . . .

Schittert het schip tussen mateloze schubben,
Slingert het schip naar zijn kolkende bestemming,
Slingert de diepte zich om uitzinnige borsten heen,
Schittert de diepte als sidderend hart.

4

Quivering with a tail
On its back, eyes
That see two lips.

Where the flower shows her beauty . . .

The ship glistens between extravagant scales,
The ship gets hurled to its seething destination,
The deep hurls itself around delirious breasts,
The deep glistens like a quivering heart.

5

Plotseling laten de elementen hun ingewanden gaan.
Formidabele lichtflitsen markeren de route naar de haven.
De geur van losse haren is fabelachtig en onontkoombaar.
Het schip vaart de splitsing der werkelijkheden tegemoet,
Vaart door geruisloze feiten en feiten die gorgelen.
Alle feiten zijn hier bijeen om woorden te kiezen,
Alle woorden zijn bijeen om dromen te maken,
Zo goed dat er geen klapperende zeilen meer zijn.

5

Suddenly the elements let go of their entrails.
Tremendous flashes of light mark the route to the harbour.
The perfume of loose hair is fabulous and inescapable.
The ship sails to where realities split asunder,
Sails through quiet facts and facts that gurgle.
All facts have gathered here to choose words,
All words have gathered to make dreams,
So good that there are no more flapping sails.

Al voor de loopplank gaan de voeten,
Van gezouten eelt, in de schoenen op de kade.
Een orgel zingt bedoelingen naar de meeuwen
En hun schitterende kleed van etensresten.
Al voor de loopplank pompt het hart
Een uiterste zekerheid door de buik.

De spiegel betovert de kompasnaald!

Met dromen duizelig in de mist van Nieuw-Caledonië,
Met handen die de pijn van een Thaise rug wassen,
Met dromen glashelder in het evenwicht van Spanje.
De vingers draaiend op de toppen van hun centrum,
De palmen wuivend langs een wenkbrauw,
De muizen dansend in de holte van de nek.

6

Even before the gangway the feet are afoot,
With salted calluses, in shoes upon the quay.
An organ sings its intentions to the seagulls
And their glistening coats of leftovers.
Even before the gangway the heart pumps
An utmost certainty through the belly.

The mirror bewitches the compass needle!

With dreams dizzy in the mist of New Caledonia,
With hands that wash the pain from a sore Thai back,
With crystal clear dreams in the balance in Spain.
The fingers turning on the tips of their centre,
The palms waving past an eyebrow,
The mice dancing in the hollow of the neck.

7

Broek met overhemd met toeterende knopen.
De transparante deining in de stenen in de wind.
Een vrouw droogt haar polsen en haar armen.
Welke droom droogt de tranen van een wolk?
De gemeenschap van woorden is een werveling
Die in ingewanden woont, en in de mond.

Kompasnaald betovert spiegel . . .

Terwijl de lippen de mond niet nodig hebben,
Terwijl de tong volle sterren dichterbij haalt
Om uiteen te zetten hoe wreed verlangen is,
Naar ooglid, schouderblad, vraag, mogelijkheid,
Terwijl de lippen van een sinaasappel proeven,
Terwijl de tong zich vurig in tweeën splitst.

7

Trousers and shirt with trumpeting buttons.
The transparent swell in the rocks in the wind.
A woman dries her wrists and her arms.
Which dream dries the tears of a cloud?
The community of words is in a whirl,
Alive in the entrails, and in the mouth.

Compass needle bewitches mirror . . .

While the lips have no need for the mouth,
While the tongue pulls closer stars that are full
So as to explain the cruelty of desire
For eyelid, shoulder blade, question, possibility,
While the lips taste of an orange,
While the tongue splits into two fiery halves.

Beste Lian, dierbare vriend, Lian, voor het zeemanshuis
Staat een lange man met blond haar die tegen een ander zegt:
In Kopenhagen, in een smerige kelder? Daar logeert de maffia.
En ik word in het leven gehandicapt door mijn dure kop.
Wat ik niet goed begrijp, zegt de ander, hoe kun jij toch
Met jouw intellect zo weinig kijk hebben op sociale processen?
Dat is yin en yang, zegt de lange, kwaad geven en goed krijgen.
Niks van aan, zegt de ander, jij moet gewoon normaal doen.

Een auto rijdt langs, de deur gaat open,
De gang is elegant, links de eetzaal,
Trap klimt gehoekt naar de volgende,
Een deur gaat open: het dominospel,
De ogen brandend, met champagne.
Lian, we waren ooit in Genua, ik telde vierhonderd straten.
Hier in Gent ben ik vingers kwijt, alleen dit glanzende dok telt.
Waar de bloem haar schoonheid toont, is de zeeman op zijn best.
Kijk, belletjes springen van trillende voeten naar vragende enkels,
Kijk, belletjes kussen de diepte tussen de juiste hoeveelheid ogen.

8

Dear Lian, my dear friend, Lian, in front of the sailor's home
A tall man with blond hair says to another:
In Copenhagen, in a grotty cellar? That's where the Mafia stays.
And I'm handicapped in life by my expensive head.
What I don't quite understand, says the other, how you
With your intellect have such little insight into social processes?
That's yin and yang, says the tall one, doing harm with kindness in return.
No way, says the other, you just have to act normal.

A car drives past, the door opens,
The passage way is elegant, on the left the dining room,
Stairs climb at right angles to the next,
A door opens: the domino game,
With burning eyes, with champagne.
Lian, once we were in Genoa, I counted four hundred streets.
Here in Ghent I'm missing fingers, only this shiny dock counts.
Where the flower shows her beauty, the sailor is at his best.
Look, a string of bells leaps from trembling feet to questioning ankles,
Look, a string of bells kisses the depth between the exact number of eyes.

De woorden op de helften van de tong
Worden zelfstandiger en onafhankelijker!
Ze beginnen elkaar dingen toe te roepen,
Ambitieus onder een oneindige hemel!
Ze doen hun best, schokkend en transparant,
Om sterren uit speeksel te destilleren!

De tas bij het raam.
De schoenen bij het raam.
De sigaretten bij het raam.
De halsketting op het bed.

Nu zijn de woorden niet meer van de tong
Maar is de tong eigendom van de woorden,
Versierde golven die enkels strelen.
De tenen maken zich los van de vloer,
Adoratie in de diepte voelen de tenen,
De tenen verspreiden roodzwart poeder,
Zacht in de lucht glijden de tenen,
De tenen laten zich zien in een wolk.

9

The words on the two halves of the tongue
Are becoming more self-reliant, more independent!
They've started crying out things to each other,
Full of zeal under an infinite sky!
They are doing their best, shaking and transparently,
To distill stars out of saliva!

The bag beside the window.
The shoes beside the window.
The cigarettes beside the window.
The necklace on the bed.

Now the words no longer belong to the tongue
But the tongue is owned by the words,
Embellished waves that stroke the ankles.
The toes disengage themselves from the floor,
Adoration is felt in the deep by the toes,
The toes diffuse red and black powder,
Softly through the air the toes are sliding,
The toes show themselves in a cloud.

Waar de bloem haar schoonheid toont,
Maakt het verlangen zich los van later,
Hangen namen in twee trossen van acht,
Krast een nagel de horizon in de huid.

Waar de bloem haar schoonheid toont
Gaan vingers over in hier en hier en hier,
Grijpen handen in sluiers van haar,
Ademen kleuren oneindig het oneindige.

Waar de bloem haar schoonheid toont
Zoemen insekten in onverstaanbaar licht,
Overschrijden ogen de bedwelmde buik,
Ruikt de onderarm vergeten dromen.

Waar de bloem haar schoonheid toont
Inspireert de medeklinker de klinker.

Waar de bloem haar schoonheid toont
Nemen vlinders het zout van de zee.

Waar de bloem haar schoonheid toont
Emailleert de tijd tatouages op blaadjes.

Where the flower shows her beauty,
Desire disengages itself from later,
Names are suspended in two bunches of eight,
A nail scratches the horizon into skin.

Where the flower shows her beauty
Fingers cross over into here and here and here,
Hands grasp at veils made of hair,
Infinite breaths give colour to infinity.

Where the flower shows her beauty
Insects hum in unintelligible light
Eyes cross the intoxicated belly,
The underarm savours forgotten dreams.

Where the flower shows her beauty
The consonant inspires the vowel.

Where the flower shows her beauty
Butterflies take the salt from the sea.

Where the flower shows her beauty
Time enamels tattoos on petals.

W.N. Herbert

W.N. Herbert was born in Dundee, Scotland, in 1961. He studied at Brase-
nose College, Oxford, where he did a BA in English Literature and then
a D.Phil. His thesis was published as *To Circumjack MacDiarmid* (OUP,
1992). He writes poetry in both English and Scots. His verse was described,
memorably, by Fiachra Gibbons in *The Guardian* as 'a weird mix of Desperate
Dan, MacDiarmid and Dostoyevsky'. *Forked Tongue*, his 1994 collection,
was shortlisted for the T S Eliot Prize and the Saltire Society Scottish Book
of the Year Award. *Cabaret McGonagall* (1996) won a Scottish Arts Council
Book Award and was shortlisted for the Forward Poetry Prize. *The Laurelude*
(1998) won a Scottish Arts Council Book Award and was a Poetry Book
Society Recommendation. His most recent collection *The Big Bumper Book
of Troy* appeared in 2002. Herbert is also the co-editor of the anthology
Strong Words: Modern Poets on Modern Poetry (2002). He is Senior Lecturer in
the School of English Literature, Language and Linguistics at the University
of Newcastle upon Tyne.

Sailors Home

Between the camouflage bar, the tattoo parlour and
        the tool shop: 'Sailors Home' in brassy
        Courier Old Victorian Orphanage font
above the now-moored gate, the bewildered mail
        washed up on its checkboard tiles
between the arches faced with black-speckled pink marble diamonds
        meeting in the features of Poseidon blurred
        by exhaust fumes on the corner of Dock Street
and Candle Row, plants growing from its grey guttering out –
grey sandstone ship departing, showing us
its high-hipped arse of galleon, its back to the firth
        as if it set sail for the Seagate instead,
        ploughing through the toun,
        closing something in the face of memory.

At its waterline in place of anchor
        the lily and the urn of municipal Dundee,
the date as chain, 1881, and
        in place of scuppers, two old sea-devil eagles
        with barnacle beards.
The pavement scarcely breaks into a wave,
        just the cracked glass tiles that let light in
        to a basement where laundry, cooking, stores
        all might have once been kept, now gone to green:
the moss a mimic of the dull dark depths they slept beside
as though they brought that heavy mistress back
and stored her in this temporary dwelling with
        its weed-dark green paintwork and
        the tropical sea-squirts, the coral letters
        of old graffiti on the Chapel door.

The cabins ascend as bleary as the weariness
        that once looked out, sinking behind their glass –
one floor filled to its dark eyelids with demarara rum;
another with the rubbery coils of oil-streaked ejaculate;
and one has a giant sucker placed to each dusty pane:
        two pale blue eyeballs fill the corner rooms –
one looking at the Custom House as though it was a language

it can no longer speak;
the other through
        the ghost of the Royal Arch like a pince nez, seeking out
the Bass Rock lightship like a lobster boiled in the docks,
that sent the Ferry lifeboatmen
        to kick their slowing boots upon the bottom of the sea;
the Unicorn, whose figurine, half hippogryph half narwhal,
it can almost understand,
that mastless training ship, deck roofed over
        as though tar had been applied to stumps.

And at the soft stone rail the two men hunching in their sculpted oilskin hats:
        twins of the doldrums and the hollowing, troughs the size
        of whole villages they lived in once,
        calms the size and age of forests cleared for sheep,
last ambassadors from that liquid city that covers the rifts between the plates,
        its catacombs that hold whole fleets of harvest,
mausolea of the piss-poor masses, slaves and whalers,
        serving-men and sons of the nobility of less nations than
there are waves to cover them;
spreaders of the cold molasses mattress
that rows them in and lets them sink.

And round the broken handrail the names of admirals
whose deeds we knew or never knew as well as fingernails
        in hands that have grown wrinkles now that won't dry out
        or knew but can't remember like green glass
        too long in sea to quite see through –
names that begin to break and flake and float away:
Nelson   Cook   Blake
      Wood   Duncan
          ?Dibdin   Napier
             Hardy   Dea_
                 Hall   An_ _ n

A Midsummer Light's Nighthouse

1

In Winter the Old High Light speaks
the language of the sea winds
and the hail: cold unwraps itself, sheet
after sheet, around its weeping edge.

In the spring it rediscovers sunlight,
lets the clouds peel off like gulls
from its lead-lidded eyeball. The earth wind mouths
against the landing door, yammering and keen.

But in the simmer-dim and dark it talks
in its own dialect: sudden as a stairwell
and silent as a corridor when the light-switch
flicks, it tells me how to listen.

2

Where do you think the music comes up from,
manifested in the taut ropes ringing
off masts of fishing boats, the grunt of motors rippling
like a fat moon's dribble on the river
and the knocking tread that's boxes, dropped upon the quays?

Where do you think the music groups itself
before the year turns over in the night?
It's propped against these timbers like a giant lens;
it's like a sunfish that's warmed itself in top waters
the eye flashing as it rolls away and drops.

3

It is by how we translate silence that
the dead become retongued: listen to
this empty air that fills two centuries
and more of chamber with the dreaming crush
of families: how it holds the creases in
their faces, how it's poised between their breaths.

4

Let the admiral slither from
his pedestal, turned from guanoed marble to
white walrus, a crawling beluga,
and pipe in his ship-whistle voice canary songs
of old calamities, wars dissolving on water.

Let the smuggler woman come
in her jellyfish petticoats, ribbons fouled with sons,
smearing the walls with rum-thickened venom,
and slur in old tobacco tones her press-gang blues,
her welcoming couplets like cold thighs.

5

The sea does not bring forth in Autumn
like an orchard – it draws back
like a page that's pinched for turning.
We read in it abeyance, not a swell.

Therefore the mind exerts its right
to halt the story, poise us on this sill
before the river sweeps the chimes away
and buries yet another solstice out at sea.

These other lives that surged before us,
let them be the gap before this midnight's tick:
our own no more inhabitable void succeeds it,
and the High Light is our common home.

Shanty of the Sailors' Moon

Mare Silentium
is whaur aa sowels at last dae come
whas life wiz spent upon
thi silent craft o song
tae sail awa sae dumb
(Mare Silentium)
we sail awa sae dumb

Layin thi keels o phrase
or sailin skeely thru the waves
that waash ower in crazy praise
until oor time is duin
and we sail tae kingdom come
(Mare Silentium)
we sail tae kingdom come

Oceans o lusty sang
atween thi lends o ports we panged
until thi saut they crehd
garred aa thi seas rin dreh
whaur we noo sail sae numb
(Mare Silentium)
we sail awa sae dumb

Tarrin thi stanza's hull
barque or ark, we tack or scull
nae hope o haven here
and sae nae need tae steer
jist sail sail tae kingdom come
(Mare Silentium)
we sail tae kingdom come

Yirth wi her bonny sash
looks doon upon a sea o ash
whaur aa ships come tae wreck
sae we waulk an eemis deck
and sail awa sae dumb
(Mare Silentium)
we sail tae kingdom come

Uwe Kolbe

with English translations by Mick Standen & Jo Tudor

Uwe Kolbe was born in East Berlin in 1957 to a family that sailed the inland waterways. He was raised in East Berlin, undertook military service after leaving school in 1976, and first published his poetry in the journal *Sinn und Form* in June 1976. In 1980-81 he undertook a course at the Johannes R. Becher Literary Institute in Leipzig, the GDR's leading centre for the study of poetics and creative writing. Between 1982 and 1985 he was banned from publishing because of anti-regime statements, particularly one in acrostic form in a poem, which the censors had failed to notice. He survived this period by taking up literary translation. From 1982-1987 he published the magazine *Mikado* with Lothar Trolle and Bernd Wagner. In 1985 he was granted a visa which permitted him to travel to western Europe and the USA. From the summer of 1988 he lived in exile in Hamburg, but returned to Berlin in 1993. From 1997-2004 he was Director of the Literature and Theatre Studio at the University of Tübingen, and has since returned to live in Berlin. Uwe Kolbe has held guest lectureships at the Universities of Texas at Austin, Vienna and Essen, and has been awarded a number of important prizes. Aside from his six collections of poetry (see page a), he has also published *Vaterlandkanal* (a travel book, 1990), *Die Situation* (1994), *Renegatentermine* (essays, 1998), *Der Tote von Belintasch* (detective story, 2002) and *Thrakische Spiele* (detective novel, 2005).

Sailor's Home
(Gedichte von Liebe und Trunkenheit)

1 Sailor's Missing

Ich habe ihn Jahre gesucht.
Ich wusste, er wohnt in der Flasche,
das war leicht festzustellen,
doch wo beginnen zu suchen?
Die Welt eine Flasche, die Flasche die Welt,
bauchig, schön, und innen drinnen,
da hat sie sich gewaschen.
Lübecker *Rotspon*
oder schwerer Argentinier?
Sherry vom Schwarzen Mann
oder Chardonnay vom Tafelberg?
Ich wusste etwas über sein Aussehen,
den Bauch.
Ich wusste um seine Meinung:
Prost auf die Welt!
Und ich wusste, ich halte zu ihm.
In Casablanca verlor sich die Spur,
dann auf dem blauen Nil,
in Schanghai,
in den Tränen des Mädchens,
dem er die Raddampferfahrt
von Dresden nach Pirna versprochen hatte,
der Luftikus, der gottverdammte
Luftikus,
da tauchte er wieder auf,
sein Buddelschiff *Made in China*.

Sailor's Home
(poems of love and drunkenness)

1 Sailor's Missing

For years I have sought him.
I knew that he lived in a bottle,
that was soon established,
though where to begin looking?
The world's a bottle, a bottle's the world,
bulging, beautiful
and it cleans itself out —
Rotspon from Lübeck
or heavy Argentinian?
That sherry with the black man on it
or Chardonnay from Table mountain?
I had some idea of his appearance,
that bulk.
I knew about his outlook:
Cheers to the world!
And I knew I had to stand by him.
The trail went cold in Casablanca
but then on the Blue Nile,
in Shanghai,
in the tears of the young girl
he'd promised to take from Dresden to Pirna
on a paddle steamer,
vapour brain, the goddamned
vapour brain
just turned up again
on board his model ship *Made in China.*

2 Sailor's Love

Mit ruhigen Schnitten löste sie
die Reste vom Kerngehäuse
aus jedem der Schnitze
des saftigen Apfels.

Ich legte mich in ihre Hand
und legte mich in ihre Ruhe.
Ich legte mich fast
in ihr Leben.

Dann stand sie wieder auf
und griff nach der Klinke
und ging zurück
in die Küchen der Welt.

2   Sailor's Love

With calm snips she removed
remnants of the core
from every slice
of the juice-filled appple.

I laid myself down in her hand
laid myself in her calm,
laid myself more or less
in her life.

But then she arose
and reached for the doorknob
and went back out
into the world's kitchens.

3   Sailor's Not Waiting

Warten kann ich nicht.
Laufen kann ich, gehen,
kommen kann ich zu dir.
Aber nicht warten, bitte
lass mich nicht warten,
unklare Zeiten, Züge,
Pläne, die mir unbekannt,
all diese objektiven
Hindernisse, bitte, vergiss,
lass mich nicht warten,
so viel steht nicht in der Zeitung,
soviel John Ashbury lesen
kommt mir nicht gut vor,
warten, das liegt mir nicht,
lieber liege ich neben dir
oder noch anders
liege ich lieber mit dir,
aber auch frühstücken
würde ich lieber mit dir
als nur auf dich zu warten
bis fast der Tag vorbei,
kann ich partout nicht,
hörst du? liest du?
nein, du kannst doch nicht lesen
jetzt, in deinem Zug vielleicht,
wissend, ich warte,
zögern kannst du doch nicht
einzusteigen, wissend,
hier ist der eine, der wartet
ohne warten zu können,
gib mir ein Zeichen,
schon lauf ich los
oder ich nehme ein Mittel,
das *beamt* oder die Tram
hier in der großen Stadt, ja,
Straßenbahnfahren ist sinnlich,
ähm sinnvoll, wenn es das Warten
abbricht und mich zu dir

3   Sailor's Not Waiting

Waiting I can't be doing with.
Running yes, walking,
getting myself to you.
but not waiting, please
don't keep me waiting,
puzzling timetables, trains,
plans unfamiliar,
all these objective
hindrances, forget the lot,
don't keep me waiting,
there's not that much in newspapers,
reading John Ashbury all the time
is not good for the health,
waiting just doesn't suit me,
I'd sooner lie next to you
or something else,
like to lie with you,
but even more
have breakfast together,
than just wait about for you
until the day's almost gone,
that really is *de trop* for me.
Hearing me? Reading me, are you?
No, you can't be reading
now, perhaps in your train
knowing I wait,
you cannot be hesitating
to arrive, knowing
here's someone waiting
who cannot wait,
give me just one sign
and I'll get going,
get myself beamed up or get a tram
here in the huge town, yes
going by tram feels real good,
well – meaningful, cutting short
this waiting, gets me to you,
lifts the weight of this Waiting

bringt, aufhebt das Warten,
dessen Opfer ich bin,
Opfer des großen Wartens,
göttlichen Wartens,
das ich nicht aushalt,
dazu bin ich viel zu klein,
auf dich zu warten, Göttin
hier in dem Tempel des Wartens,
den du geweiht hast
ohne ihn je zu betreten,
siehe ich warte, und
warten kann ich nicht.

whose victim I am,
victim of infinite waiting,
divinely ordained waiting
which cannot be borne
by someone as little as me
awaiting you, Goddess
here in the Temple of Waiting
that you have consecrated
without ever setting foot in it,
see I am waiting and
I don't do waiting.

Weißt du mein Freund, was das ist,
unendliche Traurigkeit?
Unter neuen Freunden zu sitzen,
die alten vermissen?
Lange Gespräche, ja, zu genießen,
die so verlaufen könnten oder auch anders?
Mit einer Vermutung kommen,
sie schweigend wieder mitzunehmen?
Eine alte Geschichte erzählen,
auf die es nur höfliche Nachfrage gibt?
Ein Lachen zu ernten,
das ein wenig dem Lachen gleicht,
das einmal gelacht wurde?
Unter Gleichgesinnten zu sitzen,
die deine Erfahrung nicht teilen,
nur gleichen Sinnes sind, behaupten sie,
und du willst es gerne glauben?
Weißt du, mein Freund, was das ist?

4 Sailor's Feeling Old

Do you know, my friend, what it's like,
an unending state of sorrow?
Sitting around with new friends
and missing all the old ones?
Long conversations, yes enjoyable
but they could be taking us anywhere?
Coming with a supposition,
keeping clammed up, taking it back home?
An old story when retold
arousing only polite reaction?
Getting a laugh
that's just a tiny bit
like they used to laugh?
Sitting among the like-minded
who do not share your experience,
just say that they think as you do,
and you wanting to believe them?
Do you know what it's like, my friend?

5 Sailor's Language Lesson

Es war in der Kleinstadt,
kann sein, sie war lächerlich,
du nahmst sie wie jede ernst,
weil dieses Leben nur eins ist
nach deiner bescheidenen
Rechnung.

Es kam, wie es immer kommt.
Du lerntest die Sprache der Frau
von Frage zu Frage genauer.
Ihr hattet einander erkannt
als nur zu diesem Gespräch
geboren.

Es war in der Kleinstadt,
der wirklich lächerlichen Stadt,
dass du dich eingelassen hast
und Antwort gabst
ihrem Mund, ihrem Schoß
und den Tränen.

Nach einem Kassensturz
musstest du weiterziehen,
schriebst ihr noch Karten
in eurer vertrauten Sprache,
längst sprach dein Mund
die nächste.

5   Sailor's Language Lesson

Once in a little town
which might have been ludicrous
but which like everywhere you took in earnest
because we have only one life
according to your humble
opinion.

All went along as usual.
You learned a woman's language
precisely question to question.
Two recognising each other
in this conversation,
made for it.

Once in a little town,
a really ludicrous town,
you got yourself involved
and gave answer
to her mouth and to her sex
and her tears.

But after closing for business
you had to move on,
writing her postcards
in your private language
long after your mouth
was speaking the next.

Und wieder ein Liebesgedicht
vom Rande der Katastrophen
(war's terroristischer Mord?
war's Flut und war's Hunger
oder schlicht
Shareholder's Value?).
Wir hatten anderes gelernt
und anderes versprochen
in einem der vorigen Leben,
unter dem Segel Hoffnung
im Industriezeitalter,
im Atomzeitalter,
im Ismus im Ismus im Ismus.
Was bleibt aber,
ist ein Liebesgedicht,
kleines, beharrliches Lied,
fast nichts.

6 Sailor's All

And again a love poem
from the sidelines of catastrophes
(was it terrorist murder?
inundation, famine
or simply
a stock-market slump?)
We had learnt of different things,
been promised other
in one of our former lives
under sail with hope
in the era of industrialisation,
in the Atomic Age,
in this that and the other times.
But what stays
is a love poem,
a little insistent song —
almost nothing.

7   Sailor's Midnight

Nach Monaten wieder zu Hause.
Für paar Wochen wäre schön,
sieht aber nicht danach aus.
Die Waschmaschine schleudert,
hoffentlich wachen die Nachbarn
nicht auf, die ich nicht kenne,
obwohl ich schon über ein Jahr
hier wohne; doch was heißt
wohnen? Manchmal
allein Musik zu hören,
die ich wirklich mag,
ganz leise, ganz leise?

7 Sailor's Midnight

After months away, back home again.
For a few weeks very nice,
but that's not how it looks.
The washing-machine's on spin,
hopefully not waking up the neighbours
not that I'd say I know them
even though it's more than a year
I've lived here; what does 'live'
mean? Sometimes
alone, listening to music
which I really like
with the volume right down.

Aus einem tiefen Grund heraus zu schreien,
gilt nicht als fein, es kommt nicht in die Tüte
in unserm großen Einkaufsparadies,
auf unserm Kontinent der wahren Werte.

Es gilt als unfein, kommt nicht in die Tüte,
was aus dir bricht im ungebremsten Fall,
obwohl du diesen Fall zugleich gestaltest,
den Schrei so wie gewohnt recht modulierst.

In unserm großen Einkaufsparadies,
da küsst die Freiheit in den bunten Läden
den Zwang, und beide halten sich die Waage,
die schließlich einen fairen Preis anzeigt.

Auf unserm Kontinent der wahren Werte
prangt doch auf jedem Schrei sein Preis, erst recht,
wenn er aus einem tiefen Grund herkommt.
Der Kenner schätzt das Echte als das Schöne.

Out of the Depths O Lord I cry . . .
is not civil, does not fit the trolley
in this, our great shopping paradise,
in our continent of true values.

Seen as uncivil, no one will buy
what breaks out in unguarded moments,
although these outbursts are given shape,
the cry as usual modulated fittingly.

In this our great shopping paradise
freedom and addiction kiss in colourful display,
both weigh equally on the scales
and show a fair price in the end.

Our continent of true values
highlights the price of every cry, most
when it comes out of the depths:
connoisseurs treasure the genuine as beautiful.

Erst war es beim Fado
in Porto, am Fuße der Brücke,
am Wasser des Douro.
Wir tranken schweren Portwein.

Kaum später Flamenco,
Toledo, Gewitter,
vom Wasser des Tajo umzingelt.
Nur einen Sherry genommen.

Und, logisch, Tango
damals in Buenos Aires
am trägen Rio de la Plata.
Es war ein Malbec aus Mendoza.

Einmal der Blues, der so hieß,
im Norden Chicagos
am meergroßen See.
Mit Tränen im Bier.

Der immerwährende Beat
steht in Hamburg,
das Wasser der Alsterfleete,
ein trockener Kümmel.

Ein Schiff wird kommen
in Magdeburg-Sudenburg,
am Elbe-Hafenbecken
mit einer Flasche Wermut.

La Paloma
in Birkenwerder nahe Berlin
am Briesesee.
Ein Weinbrand oder zwei.

Ein Psalm
in Budapest im Januar,
die Kettenbrücke, die Donau,
Marillenbrand (Pálinka).

First it was the Fado
in Porto, down by the bridge,
of the River Douro.
We drank heavy port-wine.

Later comes Flamenco,
Toledo, thundery,
wound in by the Tajo.
Only had a single sherry.

By logic the Tango
sometime in Buenos Aires,
by the sluggish Rio de la Plata.
The wine was Malbec of Mendoza.

Once the so-called Blues
in northern Chicago
by the sea-sized lake.
With tearful beer.

Never-ending 'Beat' music —
that was Hamburg
by the channels of the Alster.
A dry caraway schnapps.

Some Day My Boat Will Come,
Was Magdeburg-Sudenburg,
The Elbe Basin
And vermouth by the bottle.

La Paloma
on Birch Island near Berlin
in Lake Briese.
A brandy or two.

A Psalm
in January Budapest,
the Chain Bridge, the Danube,
apricot brandy (Palinka).

Das Volkslied, Dudelsack,
im uralten Plovdiv,
das flache Bett der Mariza
und schwerer Mavrud.

Einmal ein Choral,
in Tübingen
am schifflosen Neckar.
Mit Messwein.

Folksong and Bagpipes
in ancestral Plovdiv,
the low bed of the Mariza
and heavy Mavrud.

And once even a chorale
in Tübingen
by the shipless Neckar.
Holy communion wine.

Wir müssen aufhören.
Es ist Frühling, und wir müssen aufhören.
Wie alles aufhört, wir müssen so
aufhören, wie alles aufhört.
Ich habe deinen Brief nicht gelesen.
Wir müssen aufhören.
Wir tun einander weh.
Es ist Frühling, und wir tun einander weh.
Alles hört auf. Im Frühling beginnt
der Kreislauf erneut. Wir müssen
aufhören, müssen wir, wir.
Wir also, das Wir hört auf.
Das ist keine feierliche Erklärung.
Es ist fürchterlich. Es tut weh.
Es tut aber weniger weh, als wir
einander weh tun, wenn wir nicht
aufhören. Wo wir nicht nur einander,
wo wir auch anderen weh tun,
weh getan haben, wenn das Aufhören
beginnt, wenn wir das können.
Das Wir hört auf, weil wir aufhören.
Wir haben das Vermögen, die Kraft.
Ich habe deinen Brief nicht gelesen.
Wir können aufhören.
Wir können sogar im Frühling,
wenn, wie immer im Frühling,
alles beginnt, in so einem Moment
können wir aufhören.
Das ist gut, das ist sehr gut.
Das tut nicht weh.
Es hört auf.

We really have to stop.
It's Spring, and we must really stop.
Everything ends and we must
stop like everything else.
I have not read the letter you sent.
We really have to stop.
We are hurting one another.
It is Spring and we're hurting each other.
Everything ends. In Spring the cycle
starts anew. We must,
must, must stop.
Us also, that 'us' will stop.
That is not a formal declaration.
It's horrible. It causes pain.
It does less hurt than it would
to each other, if we didn't
stop. Not just us it hurts
but causes pain to others
and hurts as the stopping
starts, if we can
the 'us' will cease when we stop.
We do have the power, the strength.
I didn't read your letter.
We can stop, stop
even in the Spring
when everything is beginning again
as it does; even at such a time
we can stop.
That's good, very good.
It does not hurt, it
stops.

Peter Laugesen

with English translations by Anne Born

Peter Laugesen was born in 1942. Expelled from the Situationist International for being a poet in 1963, he has since concentrated his revolutionary activities around poetry. In addition to his more than 50 books since *Landskab*, published underground in 1967, he has worked with poetry as painting ("writing on the wall"), as music and theatre, and has also translated Antonin Artaud, Heiner Müller, Gunnar Björling, Charles Olson, Georg Büchner, Heinrich von Kleist, Peter Handke, Novalis, William Shakespeare and others.

en endeløs række
af flasker beholdere tømt
er havet

sten og støv

figurer

døren åben
til den våde nat

dynger af lyd

        the sea
    is an endless raft
of empty bottles and containers

            stones and dust

                    figures

                        the door open
                        onto the wet night

                    heaps of sound

Sømand

Han snublede
over en opstreg
og drattede
ned i et blækhus

Det var koldt
og mørkt

Der var fyldt
med krav
uden mening

Han var en lille fyr
der gjorde sit bedste

Hans skib er en træklods
og masten et søm

Han har strikket et sejl
af stribede rester

Det er hans hav
der sejler han ud

Sailor

He stumbled
over an upstroke
and flopped down
into an inkwell

It was cold
and dark

It was filled
with meaningless
demands

He was a little guy
who did his best

His ship is a wooden block
with a nail for its mast

He has knitted a sail
out of striped remnants

It is his sea
He will sail out there

Landkrabbe

Jeg kender ikke noget til havet
min robåd ligger i højt græs ved søen
Det er ti år siden jeg sidst
sad på den og drak en øl
Måske skulle jeg bare lige så stille
lægge den ud på bunden
før den bliver ædt op af tid

Landlubber

I don't know anything about the sea
my upturned boat lies by the lake in tall grass
It's ten years since I last
sat on it with a beer
Maybe I should just ever so quietly
let it sink down on the bottom
before it's eaten up by time

Natdamper

Digtere er sprogets sømænd de glemmer aldrig
De siger farvel på kajen og vender ryggen til
De går om bord på færgen og vinker ikke
Man ser dem aldrig igen og det gør ondt
Det er for evigt og man glemmer dem snart
Men de glemmer aldrig for blæk er det store hav
De ligger på øverste dæk og stirrer op
I stjernerne fra en bænk med redningsbælter
De har lukket den op og set den er tom
De hører skramlende rock and roll rumstere
Under salonmusikken to dæk længere nede
De drikker med handelsrejsende i salonen
Og lytter til bølger af fortvivlet sjofle historier
Men de bor aldrig i kahyt kommer aldrig ned
I gangene med de plettede røde tæpper
De stiger af på en anden kaj og forsvinder i sne
Men de glemmer aldrig for digtet er
En ubrudt streg og slynget færd fra det første blækhus
Til pennen løber tør og skriften løber ud
Hvor alting er for evigt på dækket under stjernerne
Der sover sprogets sømand og digtet er en færge
På blodets sorte hav hvor den damper hid og did

Night Steamer

Poets are the sailors of language they never forget
They bid farewell on the quay and turn their backs
They go on board the ferry without waving
You never see them again and that hurts
It is for ever and you'll soon forget them
But they never forget for ink is the great ocean
They lie on the top deck gazing up
At the stars from a bench stuffed with lifebelts
They have opened it and seen it is empty
They hear the rattle and din of rock 'n roll
Beneath the saloon music two decks below
They drink with commercial travellers in the saloon
And listen to waves of despairing smutty stories
But they never sleep in cabins never go down
In the corridors with their stained red carpets
They go ashore at a different quay and vanish in snow
But they never forget for the poem is
An unbroken line hurled out from the first inkwell
Until the pen runs dry and the writing runs out
Where everything is for ever on the deck under the stars
Where the sailor of language sleeps and the poem is a ferry
On the black sea of blood where it steams ever and on

Den Store Bog

Egen er tung af lys
og skrevet med blyant
ud fra bredden

Vinden bladrer
i rytmiske pust
gennem dens blade

En dag vil en sidste
stormfuld læser
blæse den hen
over søens spejl

The Great Oak Book

The dug-out is heavy
with light and written in pencil
out from the shore

The wind
ruffles its leaves
with rhythmic breaths

One day a last
stormy reader
will blow it away
over the mirror of lakes

En båd er et vandrende hus
af brædder i spænd
mellem øer og skær

Endeløst sejler den
hjem skal den ikke

Der findes et sted
i dens bankende hjerte
hvor alting engang er begyndt

På bunden af søen
findes det væld
der holder den fuld

A boat is a travelling house
of interlocking boards
between islands and skerries

Endlessly it sails
It cannot go home

There is a place
in its beating heart
where everything once began

At the bottom of the lake
is the fount
that keeps it full

Jolly Roger

Der er flasken den skal tømmes
så først kan de krogede fingre
fumle med tændstikker lim og strik
Skibet skal bygges bjælke for bjælke
fregatten skal sejle den skal i flasken
rigningen rejses med fiskesnøre
på strittende master hvor drømmens sømænd
kan kravle og lange John Silver humpe
ned i kabyssen efter en ny flaske rom
før et nyt skib kan bygges
John Silver henter hver gang den næste
til bølgerne vugger det sidste i mørket
der står som blæk ind mod hans vindue
ud mod en gade hvor blinde kaptajner
stirrer på dødningeflag i rækker af spejle

Jolly Roger

There is the bottle it must be emptied
before the crooked fingers can fumble
with matches glue and cord
The ship must be built plank by plank
the frigate must sail it has to get in the bottle
the rigging hoisted with fishing line
on straight masts where the sailors of dream
can climb and Long John Silver hobble
down to the galley for a new bottle of rum
before a new ship can be built
Each time John Silver fetches the next one
until the waves rock the last ship into the darkness
pressing like black ink against his window
onto a street where blind captains
gaze at the skull and crossbones through rows of mirrors

Normandie

Markise, Deres striber
ned mod stranden op mod solen
er en slikkepind for sjælen,
og de svarer liggestolen
når den blafrer lidt i vinden,
når den aer Dem på kinden. Markise,
Deres pudder står i tågeslør mod aften,
alt det sludder folk kan pruste
når de står med boblesaften,
ser på himlen fra altaner
børn der leger blandt plataner,
ser på sejl i horisonten
store linere på vej
der står stille i en lomme
af en tid, der snart vil komme. Deres nærvær,
Markise, som et minde om en verden
fuld af løgn, af sorg og sødme.

Det franske atlanterhavsskib *Normandie*, 83.423 bruttotons, blev søsat i 1933 og havde sin jomfrurejse i 1935. Det skød en fart af 28,5 knob. Det brændte i februar 1942 ved tysk sabotage i New York og blev ophugget i 1947.

Normandie

Marquise, your stripes running down
to the beach and up to the sun
are a lollipop for the soul,
and they answer the deck chair
as it flutters slightly in the wind
where it honours your cheek. Marquise,
at evening your powder is a veil of mist
all the rubbish people can come out with
when they stand with their bubbly
and scan the sky from balconies
children playing among plane trees
watch sails on the horizon
great liners on their way
standing still in a pocket
of time that is to come. Your presence,
Marquise, like a memory from a world
full of lies, of sorrow and sweetness.

The French Atlantic liner *Normandie*, 83,423 tonnes, was launched in 1933 and made her
maiden voyage in 1935. She had a top speed of 28.5 knots. In 1942 she was burned out in
New York by German arsonist saboteurs and was broken up in 1947.

Sømandens hjem er
det sorte skib
der sejler ham hjem når han dør

Det letter anker
på drømmenes red
og fugle følger ham bort

De sætter kurs
gennem fiskens øje
mod stjernernes tomme net

The sailor's home is
the black ship
that sails him home when he dies

It weighs anchor
in the roadstead of dreams
and birds trail in his wake

They set a course
through the fish's eye
for the empty net of the stars

Det er kun
et lille skrammelskib
i himmelrummet.

It is nothing but
a small scrap heap of a ship
in the vault of heaven.

Sømandens blues

jeg er
en burre af skrald
hængt på vind
alle helst vil slukke
jeg er
en posemand til robotten
når det lys tændes
der afsøger kroge
for tomme æsker
jeg er
en løs kanon
på et synkende skib

The Sailor's Blues

I am
a burr of garbage
hung on wind
everyone wishes
will drop
I am
a dustman for the robot
when the light is lit
that searches corners
for empty boxes
I am
a loose cannon
on a sinking ship

Karine Martel

with English translations by Vivienne Vermes

Karine Martel was born in France in 1968, has lived in Australia, Thailand and Indonesia, and is now based in Paris. Trained as a classical dancer, she studied philosophy after suffering a serious accident. She has two children.

She published her first collection of poems, *Textures*, in 2001 and followed this with two further collections *Franchir la peau* and *Poème pour un marin*, both in 2004. Each of these books also features the work of the photographer, Vincent Hart. In 2004, her first novel *Après* appeared. All of her work is published by Éditions Caractères, Paris.

Forthcoming work: a collection of ten poems on ten Sébastien Mayor sculptures will appear in December 2005, and a book written jointly with Arjen Duinker, *Et cela? L'infini*, will be published by Querido, Amsterdam in January 2006. Karine Martel is also currently working on a novel, *Les recluses*, and another collection of poems, *Les cerfs-volants*, the latter again with the collaboration of Vincent Hart. The poems from *Sailor's Home* will also appear in Dutch translation in the journal *De Revisor*.

Sailor's Home

I

La mer s'est retirée et a laissé le monde
Vide
Dans une anse de silence
Dans un instant fossile
Vide
Sur la dune absorbée
Sur les algues galiciennes.

Les barques ont le ventre à l'air
Et digèrent le varech sous les étoiles
Du reflux.

La parole s'est perdue
Dans une vasque asséchée
Les pieds seuls saignent et crissent
De courir dans le sable acide pour éviter
L'afflux.

Prenons le large! La marée s'est épuisée dans le désert.

Le tarissement s'en vient aux commissures
Les langues s'échancrent
Les encres se mêlent
Le monde s'enfle
D'une rumeur en rebond
D'une pulsation de l'ascèse
Du cycle des heures mortes.

Prenons le vide! Avec la marée des paroles émaciées.

Sailor's Home

I

The sea receded and left the world
Void
In a bay of silence
In an instant a fossil
Void
On the absorbed dune
On the Galician seaweed

The boats bare their bellies
Digest kelp under the starlit
Ebb.

The word is adrift
In a parched basin
Only the feet bleed, scratched
By the race across acid sand, to escape
The return of sea surge.

Set sail for the open sea! The tide is drained in the desert.

On the verge of dessication
Tongues part
Inks smudge
The world swells
With rumour on the rebound
With ascesis' beat
With the cycle of dead hours.

Set sail for the void! On the tide of emaciated words.

2

Les rives se rétractent en mots tactiles
Et le corps des femmes geint en cadence
Dans l'exil de l'absorption lente du vent
Des marins gémissant leur terril
Dans les torrents poreux d'une vérité
Sans rivages.
Le temps se tait avec les femmes bleues
Et l'attente commence dès l'origine.

L'amante a des douves abondantes
Mais ploie dans le ressac abrupt
Des réclusions du plaisir.

Le monde s'évide arasé de soleil
Le relent des cadavres s'estompe
Avec les algues et les poissons morts
Et les jupons de lin chargés d'argile.

Le temps encore se tait au seuil des valves
Et la bouche de sel sue de la soie
Jusqu'à la pénombre de l'éclipse.

The banks withdraw into tactile words
And the body of woman whimpers in rhythm
Exiled by the slow pull of the wind
Sailors groan their slurry
In the porous torrents
Of a shoreless truth.
Time stays silent with the blue women
And the waiting begins from the beginning.

The lover has ample moats
Yet in the sharp undertow of pleasure's retreat,
She yields.

The world a cavity flattened by the sun
The stench of corpses quenched
By seaweed and dead fish
And linen petticoats laden with clay.

Still time stays silent on the edge of the shell's hinge
And the salt mouth sweats silk
Until penumbra and eclipse.

3

Dans l'antre d'une éponge le monde s'est tapi
Le monde ou le poète, lapidaire différence,
L'un a mal au ventre l'autre mal aux pieds:
Au creux la faim des crevasses limoneuses.
L'heure chaloupe sur les berges les yeux clos . . .

La rétention communie à l'ivresse
L'épanchement met la soif en bandoulière
Les filets sont jetés dans le sillage des cuisses
Longues qui traînent derrière les barques.
L'espace est odorant et ouvre une veine . . .

L'océan afflue là où la mer se retire
Là où les femmes portent des mantilles noires
Ou des fards trop blancs ou des croix trop lourdes.
Souvent les péninsules se laissent immerger
Souvent les sirènes chantent alignées sur les murs . . .

Les enfants jouent avec les fleurs et les papillons
Et collectionnent les éponges et les yeux du destin
Trouvés dans l'or du sable à coups de pelles.
Le monde est en repos dans la tranche des livres
Et malheur à celui qui ouvre le grimoire . . .

3

The world withdraws into the sponge's inner sanctuary
The world or the poet, lapidary difference,
One aches in the stomach, the other in the foot:
In the hollow the hunger of mud-filled crevices.
Time swaggers on the steep banks eyes shut . . .

Retention and drunkenness in communion
Thirst is bundled on the back of effusion
Nets are cast in the wake of long thighs
Spread behind boats.
The space is fragrant and opens a vein . . .

The ocean flows there where the sea recedes
There where the women wear black mantillas
Or paint their faces too white, or carry crosses too heavy.
Often the peninsulas slide into the deep
Often the mermaids sing, side by side on the walls . . .

The children play with flowers and butterflies
Collect sponges and the eyes of fate
Found by the thrust of a spade in the gold of sand.
The world is at peace between the edges of pages
And woe to him who opens the book of spells . . .

Rester dans sa coque, n'est-ce pas rester dans le verbe
Et y faire la fête?
S'allonger dans la coque d'un bateau qui prend le large
Et oublier les hommes en cendres
Les illusionnistes de la division
Les pourvoyeurs de singes
Les prolixes de signes.

Epingler sur le bois des vierges enluminées,
Des cristaux chamaniques, des visages ridés,
Et brûler de l'encens dans la steppe mongole,
Puis se retourner sur sa couche avec la vague.
La pluie est mouillée de fleurs sombres
Qui tombent en diagonales dans les rêves
Des fronts durs saoulés par les hamacs.

Hypnos n'est pas loin et joue de la flûte de sureau
Et l'hiver venu mange les flocons du souvenir . . .
Un jour une Belle attendit sur la rive en tissant
Des cordages pour les singes de cendres, nuit et jour
Eclaboussée d'écume, nuit et jour conjurant
Le naufrage, humant de la terre vide les voiles
Salines et le bois vermoulu, sans larmes.

Peindre la coque, n'est-ce pas peindre le verbe
Pour y faire la fête?

4

To stay in the hull, is it not to stay in the word
And make merry?
To lie in the hull of a boat bound for the open sea
Forgetting men of ash
Magicians of division
Suppliers of monkeys
Overflowing with signs.

To pin shamanic crystals, wrinkled faces,
To the wood of illuminated virgins,
And to burn incense in the Mongolian steppes,
Then to turn in the bunk with the wave swell.
The rain is wet with dark flowers
They fall aslant in the dreams
Of harsh foreheads drunk-lulled in hammock sway.

Hypnos hovers, plays an elderberry flute
Come winter he eats the snowflakes of memory . . .
One day a Beauty waited on the bank, weaved
Weft for the monkeys of ash, night and day
Splashed with spray, night and day conjuring
The wreck, sucking salt sails and worm eaten wood
From the empty earth,
She never shed one tear.

To paint the hull, is it not to paint the word
And make merry?

5

De l'étendue rien ne reste
Microcosmes et alluvions
Vague après vague claire
Chahutés par le bruit sec
Des voiles qui claquent.

La mer est une sédimentation
De l'œil toujours en passe
De se dissoudre dans la fleur
De sel dans la panse du sort
Dans le souffle centrifuge.

C'est à l'estuaire du sens
Que se noie l'image plane
Les embruns scient l'œil
Dur en une blessure nette
D'où jaillit le sang du songe.

Ami tu es un faune aveugle
Ou une Ariane ligamenteuse
Effilochés en houle et langues
D'écume absorbés par le sable
Où tombent les étoiles.

Le poudroiement multiple
Lèche les pieds marins
Entortille les chevilles
Rafraîchit les rotules
Explose les corps compacts.

5

Nothing remains of the vast expanse
Microcosms and alluvions
Wave after clear wave
Jostled by the sharp sound
Of the sails' flap.

The sea is a sedimentation
Of the eye ever ready
To dissolve in the flower
Of salt in the belly of fate
In the centrifugal breath.

At the estuary of meaning
Here, the flat image drowns,
Spray slices the hard eye
A clean wound
That spouts the blood of dreams.

Friend, you are a blind faun
Or a ligamentous Ariadne
Frayed into sea swell and tongues
Of foam soaked up
By the starfall sand.

The myriad whirls
Lick the sealeg feet
Become ankle twine
Restore kneecaps
Explode the body's density.

6

Monte une rumeur lucide et gaie
Monte un chaos dans la salive
La chair déploie ses palmes nues
Dans les tubulures grises des coraux.

La nuit blanchit dans l'en-dehors
Pour une gorgée d'eau ils écopent
Les sources
Percent des torrents.

Le vide est pris d'assaut
La mer se rêve étale
La fleur disloque les amarres souterraines . . .

Ils marchent,
Même si le pas est mortel,
Le corps fendu par la machette,
Et décrochent les fruits phosphorescents.

La rumeur du monde monte dans la pulpe des murmures.

6

A murmur rises, bright, gay,
Chaos rises in the saliva
Flesh webs wide its feet
In the grey tubulures of coral.

In the outside, night grows pale
They bail out springs
Pierce waterfalls
For a mouthful of water.

The void is under attack
The sea slackens
The flower dislodges underground moorings . . .

They walk,
Even if footfall is fatal,
The body cleaved by the machete,
And they pluck phosphorescent fruit.

The world's murmur rises in the whispers' pulp.

7

Pour Elénore

Elle a la chevelure sauvage des manouches
Les doigts des autres restent pris dans la toile.
Elle vole des parfums en respirant les flacons:
De l'Oud venu des caves pour le passé
De la bergamote pour la soif de demain
De la rose pour le départ d'aujourd'hui.
Elle ne vole jamais que le vent humain.

Elle ne lit ni ne signe ni ne trace
Rien
Elle danse à la risée du monde
Rien
Elle danse à l'orée des rizières
Rien
Elle danse à la lisière des mers
Rien ! Rien ! Rien !
Elle est la rosée de l'onde après . . .

. . . après l'évaporation.

Après l'évaporation la terre brûle
Les gousses de vanille s'assèchent
Au fond des nasses d'osier cassant
Les visions verticales s'écoulent
Dans le fucus en poudre vert sombre.
Les peaux de serpent sont ses fourreaux
A son cou des colliers de clovisses
A ses oreilles l'écaille des tortues
Sur ses bras la carapace des crabes
Elle a aussi volé l'horizon après . . .

. . . après la réclusion.

7

For Elénore

She has the wild hair of a gypsy
The fingers of others get caught in its web.
She breathes in the flacon's fragrance
And steals its perfume:
From cellars, the waters of Oud for the past
Bergamot for the thirst for tomorrow
Rose for farewell to today.
She steals only, ever, a wind that blows human.

She neither reads nor signs nor draws
Nothing
She dances to the mockery of the world
Nothing
She dances at the edge of rice fields
Nothing
She dances at the parting of seas
Nothing! Nothing! Nothing!
She is the dew on the wave . . .

. . . after evaporation.

After evaporation the world burns
Vanilla cloves turn dry at the bottom
Of the brittle wicker of the fisherman's trap
Vertical visions flow out
Into the dark green fucus powder.
Her sheaths are snake skins
A cockle necklace around her neck
Tortoise-shells upon her ears
On her arms the carapace of crab
She stole the horizon too after . . .

. . . after reclusion.

Après la réclusion la voilà Ile
La voilà sans nom et sans port
La voilée longiligne et sans phare
Une île au nord du nord allongée
Sans langueur ni lait ni dattes
Jusqu'à la disparition d'après.

After reclusion she, now, Island,
She, now, without name or port
Veiled in sail billow, slendered, lighthouse-less,
An island north to north reclining
Without langour, or milk, or dates
Until the vanishing of after.

La mer est revenue dans un long déferlement de houle
Une houle inégale sortie de l'haleine des apatrides.
Venue d'un lieu du monde essoré elle veut parler
Des langues.
Elle ne connaît que celle du silence.
Elle a laissé l'éternité derrière elle.
Elle ne sait que la transparence.
La houle est née avec la vague du monde.
Elle veut parler d'un lieu vierge
Celui de l'instant cru
Sans les stances cycloïdales
Sans les instances des pensées.
Le long déferlement de houle est une pivoine à l'aube
Un éclatement incarnat dans une citadelle enclose.
Elle n'a ni lieu ni repos
Elle est le lieu et le repos
Elle n'a ni raison ni sens
La houle est la raison et le sens.
Elle parle la première langue puis la deuxième et la troisième
L'infini est devant elle la quatrième et la cinquième
Chaotique sans cesse elle est chez elle dans la parole nacrée.
De la nuit au jour et du jour à la nuit
Dans le vide du ciel ou le plein de l'étoile
La houle naît avec le monde et déroule les eaux
Et saccage les murailles
Et entraîne les océans
Et assassine l'interdit
Originel.

The sea's surge returns, a long surfbreak of swell
Unequal swell, breath of those disenfranchised, stateless.
Come from a place in a dried world it wants to speak
Languages.
It knows only the speech of silence.
It has left eternity behind it.
It knows only transparency.
The swell was born on the wave of the world.
It wants to speak of a virgin place
Place of the stark moment
Without cycloid stances
Without thoughts' insistence.
The long surfbreak of swell is a dawn poppy
Incarnate budburst in a closed citadelle.
It has neither place nor peace
It is place and peace
It has neither reason nor sense
The swell is reason and sense.
It speaks the first language, then second and third
Infinity lies ahead the fourth and fifth
It is at home, never ending in chaos, in the lustre of the word.
From night to day and from day to night
In the sky's void or the fullness of stars
The swell is born with the world and unleashes waters
And shatters high walls
And sweeps along oceans
And murders the first
Taboo.

9

A l'ouverture est l'impensé
sans autre refuge
la bouche
à l'embouchure du temps
le fleuve se jette
ou se trouve
ou se glisse
ou naît
encore ici
dans le désir du seuil.

Ceci de l'impensé
Cela de l'improbable
Nulle part en son abri
Le marin brûle la conjonction.

Et . . .

Renaît au verbe

Est . . .

Bouche-à-bouche au bûcher
les pores crépitent
de naître
avec la prochaine vague.

9

In the beginning is the unthought
with no other refuge
the mouth
at the opening of time
the river hurls
or finds itself
or slides
or is born
still here
in the desire for the threshold.

This the unthought
That the improbable
With no place a refuge
The sailor burns the conjunction.

And . . .

Is reborn to the word

Is . . .

Mouth-to-mouth on the stake
the pores crackle
to be born
on the next wave.

Ce n'est qu'escale ici entre deux langues de terre
Ta barque est une goélette ou un sous-marin
Les enfants aiment les vaisseaux et les caravanes
Et les tentes instables plantées dans les jardins
Et les épées de bois pour bâtir des histoires
Sur des étendues invisibles.
Leur château est le tien si tu prends pour ciboire
Le dé à coudre ou le gobelet percé et pour grand cru
L'eau claire des tuyaux d'arrosage.
Ce n'est qu'escale ici, pas une forteresse . . .

Here is simply a port of call between two tongues of earth
Your boat is a seagull or a submarine
The children like vessels and caravans
And rickety tents pitched in gardens
And swords made of wood to build stories
On invisible expanses.
Their castle is yours if you take for your ciborium
A thimble or a pierced glass and for fine wine
The clear water from a hose pipe.
Here is simply a port of call, not a fortress . . .

Yang Lian

with English translations by Brian Holton

Yang Lian was born in Switzerland in 1955, and grew up in Beijing. He began writing when he was sent to the countryside in the 70s, and on his return became one of the first group of young "underground" Chinese poets, who published the influential literary magazine *Jintian*. Yang Lian's poems became well known and influential inside and outside of China in the 1980s, especially when his long poem 'Norlang' was criticized widely by the government during the "Anti-Spiritual Pollution" campaign.

He was invited to visit Australia and New Zealand in 1988, and became an exile after the Tiananmen massacre. He has since published seven volumes of poems, two volumes of prose, and many essays in Chinese, and has been translated into more than twenty languages.

His three volumes of collected works were published by Shang Hai Wen Yi Chu Ban She (Literature and Arts Press of Shanghai); his most recent collections in English are *Yi* (Green Integer, Los Angeles, 2001), and *Concentric Circles* (Bloodaxe Books, 2005), both booklength poems.

SAILOR'S HOME

1. 春光 · 河谷

这一刻无限大　阳光裸出的身子那么大
裸着　一篷金色茸毛紧紧挤着
我们的头埋进去　河谷磨擦脸颊

这一刻　躺在怀里的是个春天的轮廓
轮到你了　闭上眼也觉得群山在下面
鸟鸣令子宫粉红幸福地收缩

风不动　五道血痕也追着五枚指尖
追上一条被你藏在羞涩里的缝
又香又软　推着绿绿的两岸

我们就看见　下次呼吸没有风景
河谷弯进光　光速在每滴水珠里崩溃
我们知道　令世界亮得晕眩的命

完成于一刹那　这一刻的心醉
亲吻这一刻的毁灭　抱紧是一朵花
抖着　勃起着　发烫的一点　就象蕊

Sailor's Home

1   Spring Scene – River Valley

this infinitely big moment   exposed by sunlight so big, this body
exposing   a mat of tightly-clustered golden down
our heads are buried in it   rubbing our cheeks a river valley

this moment   what lies embraced is the shape of spring
lined up for you   eyes closed you feel the hills are below
birdsong making your womb contract with pink blessing

wind stilled   bloodstains chasing the end of each finger
catching the crack you hide within your shyness
soft and fragrant   pushing the green banks of the river

so we see   next breath there's no scenery
river valley bends into light   lightspeed crumbling within each drop of water
we know   the destiny that makes the world bright and dizzy

complete in an instant   this enchantment
kiss the destruction of the moment   the tight hug is the flower
trembling   erect   burning   point like a pistil or stamen

2. LYN BEACH

海浪也一直在寻找　　用风暴寻找
海把尖尖挺起的乳头递到你嘴里
童年　象绷紧的帆绳那样嘶叫

象排油漆斑驳的小房子　残破倾圮
却把一只耳朵的珍珠贝留在窗台上
涛声把小名舔剩银白的骸骨时

水平线忍着呻吟　水中抽出紫丁香
涨潮就在长大　一张从未压皱的床单
叫你怕　你要又一个四月被弄脏

海滩的女性　无论怎样挪远
都有一条鱼鲜嫩的腹部　好继续学习疼
你长长的双腿盘紧这个傍晚

湿的拉力　一股拼命回头看的激情
用尽了海　肉盛满一罐哭声来到
一个黑到底的形式　才配追上你的诞生

waves have been searching all along   storm searching
sea puts a sharp standing nipple in your mouth
childhood   like an overstretched halyard squealing

like a little room mottled with exuded paint   destroyed and dilapidated
leaving the pearl shell of an ear on the windowsill
when surf licks your nickname what's left is a skeleton, silver-white, articulated

horizon surrers its groans   lilac from water pulled
so the tide is growing up   a never wrinkled bedsheet
makes you afraid   you want another April polluted

the beach's female sex   surely somehow far away shifting
with the delicate belly of a fish   to go on learning pain
your long legs twist hard around this gloaming

the pull of the wet   a desperate passion to turn and survey
has used up the sea   flesh fills a pot of sobs to arrive at
a form black all through   then it deserves to catch your birthday

3. 岸

水波粼粼作曲　不远处一架死钢琴
在潮汐中响着　死水手精心修剪的五指
摇曳　满房间白珊瑚和康乃馨

满含最后一瞥的性感　一盏烛火透视
性交的肉体中一个岸透明的结构
我们彼此是锚　彼此是锚地

蓝色动荡的家　一块皮肤就是港口
我们嵌着的缺口　炫耀大海空出的方向
死船长冷冰冰指挥一场演奏

音乐会就夹在我们大腿间　那流淌
一股血味儿　血淋淋挥舞器官的旗语
那茎指着说　没别的地方

你能去　你该去　墙上的死镜框里
一头蒙着蓝色条纹的兽慢慢逡巡
岸　记住最后一瞥　那一瞥无终无始

the waves' crystal composing   dead piano at an interval
in the sounding of the tides   dead sailor's carefully trimmed fingers
swaying   a room full of carnations and white coral

filled with the sexiness of a final stare   candle flame's x-ray visage
shore a transparent structure in the flesh of lovemaking
we are each other's anchor   we are each other's anchorage

shaky blue house   skin is the harbour
the breach inlaid in us   shows off the direction where the ocean empties
the dead captain icily conducts the overture

the concert is squeezed between our thighs   the flow
a whiff of blood   semaphore that waves bloody organs
the root says as it points   no other place to go

you can go   you should go   in the dead mirror-frame on the panelling
the beast that covers over blue clauses slowly withdraws
shore   remember the last stare   stare with no end or beginning

4. "水手之家"

一行字刻在墙上　不停出海的字
把孩子们变老了　不停疯长的蓝色花草
听小小的白眼珠在防波堤上哭泣

父亲的精液是一个异国　被一道
盛满明媚早晨的裂缝隔开
母亲　躲进海鸥茫然的啼叫

分别就再次分娩　把这团血肉遗下来
又一排小小的白浪头把远方打得更远
孩子们否认海那边有个世界

不停构思着　把阳光变黑的血缘
把岸变得狂暴　把被抛弃当作一件作品
那时间表上永不到来的时间

永远卡在　即将挤出血腥隘口的一瞬
母亲哭嚎　父亲肿胀的阴囊低垂
如星座　蠕动　孩子否认不了的命运

a line of words carved on the wall   words endlessly sailing
making children old   endlessly overgrown blue plants
on the breakwaters hear white eyeballs weeping

father's semen is a foreign land   separated by
the gap filled with radiant morning sunlight
mother   hides in the seagull's blank cry

once more separation gives birth   abandons this piece of vellum
another row of thin white waves beating far into farther
children deny that beyond the sea there is another realm

endlessly plotting   sunshine-blackening ancestry
maddening the shore   turning being forsaken into a work of art
the time that never comes is in the directory

forever blocked   at the instant that will squeeze through the bloody chimney
mother wails   father's swollen dropped scrotum hangs down
like a constellation   wriggling   children's undeniable destiny

5．午睡的海图

光在窗外倾泄　　漂过床头的白色水母
累了　半透明的室内象只半闭的眼帘
鱼类五彩的尾巴围着蜡烛

她睡在就象死在海底卵石间
死了　还梦见一丛被摆布的黑色海草
肉体那么无知　肉体持续下潜

丝丝痒的脚趾　触到嘴唇软软的珊瑚礁
化了　舌头追赶一阵脚踝上的麻
嘶嘶向里窜　一封拍往全身的电报

海香喷喷捻着一朵空间的茶花
开了　魔鬼揉弄酷似蚌肉的一小只
比她还象动物　越抽搐越湿滑

亮晶晶挣脱妄想捏拢的手指
逃了　镜子张望中　镜子还在画出
颓废的宋朝的鹤侧着身子

light floods out beyond the window   white jellyfish floating by the bed-head
tired   semi-transparent interior like a half-closed eye
dancing multi-coloured fish tailsaround the candle spread

among sea floor pebbles her sleep imitates dying
dead   still dreaming a thicket of black sea weed under orders
as ignorant as a body   a body that just goes on diving

toe's tiny itches   a soft coral reef of lips gently collide
melted   tongues chase anaesthesia on the ankles
a telegram sent to the whole body   fizzing flees inside

sea odoriferously twists a camellia of space
opened   demon rubs and plays with a small clam-like thing
more like an animal than like her   the more it skids, the more it will pulse

glistening shakes off the pinching fingers of hope that's vain
escaped   in the mirror's distant gaze   mirror still painting
lying on its side a decadent Song dynasty crane

6．午睡的海图

海面上一百万个玫瑰园泛起嫣红
床上　颈窝是精雕细刻的一小朵
别碰那乳头　让她去做梦

让两个尖　在梦中接受一种熏香的颜色
让一下午把滴滴溢出的奶噙在嘴里
此刻搂在胸前的　都是出海的

睡着　一座城市也在漂移
一双放肆的脚践踏波浪的鳞状台阶
迎向耀眼灾难的　总是一次深呼吸

满屋冉冉上升着气泡
满屋弯曲的动作　擦过被耳语提前的夜
不问也知道　小憩　正变成性交

人造的一夜中合上眼就有想要的明月
人　是块礁石收藏着结束的阴影
为抛弃存在而一股股倾泄

on the sea's surface a million flaming red rose gardens are drifting
on the bed   the hollow of the throat is a little precisely carved one
don't knock that nipple   let her go dreaming

let two tips   in dreams the perfumed colour of smoke inhale
let an afternoon hold in its mouth milk seeping out drop by drop
what this instant hugs to its breast   has all set sail

sleeping   this city too is floating off
on the scaly steps of the surf two feet run wild
what's facing dazzling disaster   is always one deep breath

the room is filled with bubbles imperceptibly rising
the flexing everywhere in the room   grazes the whisper-brought night
know without asking   a little rest   is turning into screwing

in man-made night you see the bright moon when your eyes close
man   is a reef collecting shadows of endings
pouring out in a flood to throw away existence

7．水晶宫

时代的丑陋鱼群隔着窗户一片死寂
它们的目光　扎穿石棺里那些年
翻找一枚红艳的被磨烂的阴蒂

死死纠缠的躯体上　两个极端
都插着　舌头与茎都涨成一大块水晶
塞得更满时　顶到藏得更深的终点

死死纠缠的躯体　不再回顾才透明
死过上千次的大海的卵巢
猛吸一口血　不在乎失去才怕人的硬

找到你　封存的初夜象一张初稿
黑暗象一座窗台　又摆出那盆绣球花
只让我看见　你的美已准备好

崩溃　交配的星空停进第一场大爆炸
一大团喷出的雪白没有过去
石头里走投无路的水　才抵达

a window separates from deathly stillness the ugly shoals of this time
their visions   stabbing through the years in the stone sarcophagus
rummaging for a bright red clitoris rubbed into slime

on tightly tangled bodies   doubly extreme
both inserted   both tongue and root swollen into one huge crystal
stuffed even fuller   it butts against the more deeply hidden demesne

tightly tangled bodies   only transparent if they never look back again
ovary of the ocean that thousands of times has died
violently exhales a mouthful of blood   only scarily hard if it lives with losing

finding you   sealed first night like a page first drafted
darkness like a windowsill   displays again a pot of hydrangeas
only let me see   your beauty all ready crafted

collapse   starry sky of sex stopping in the first big bang
big ball of spat-out snow white has no past
water helplessly locked in stone   has only now come along

8．复数

这个现在的复数　蓝的复数
水手漂白的身影漂浮在每道波峰上
折射成无从等待的　溺死是复数

仍自一块棱形切下水平线的　是光
仍一再改写住址的　是总嚷着还要的海
又一具射精后的尸骸被啐到石凳上

空得象海哩　绿色家俱摆满悬崖
满是时差的房间睁开有对羊眼的早晨
谁沦为无从等待的　自己不得不等待

一把水手片片削落果肉的利刃
一次都不在　却被咀嚼了无数次
一个我都不剩　才毁灭成我们

粉碎　定居在狠狠砸下的涛声里
甚至停止不了渴望一个孤独腐烂的单数
守着　摔在远方礁石上的名字

the plural of now   plural is blue
bleached shadows of sailors floating on the crests of every wave
refracted into what can't be awaited   drowning is plural too

what still cuts the horizon from the prism   is radiance
what still endlessly re-writes addresses   is the sea yelling for more
another post-coital skeleton spat out on a stone bench

it's empty as nautical miles   green furniture set out across the precipice
the room holding all time differences opens the sheep eyes of morning
who sinks into what can't be awaited   self has to wait for this

sharp blade for sailors to peel off fruit flesh in slices
doesn't once exist   though chewed times without number
not an I is left   destroyed only then to become us

shatter   domiciled in the heartless pounding surf
can't even stop longing for a lonely rotting singular
watching   a name flung on the distant reef

9．绞架上的苹果

你用整整一年想像插进自己里面的核
一根旋转的轴　一种你想否认的力
否认不了　秋天是把绞杀的文火

一个碧蓝的拎着你在空中晃的逻辑
离地几米高　涨红的果肉抱着核摩擦时
风摸你　此刻谁想摸就摸你

冷钉进内心　甜才格外放肆
腐烂有个把柄　攥住就嗅到性的腥香
你把自己挂上一枚黄金的倒刺

离世界几米高　交给最粗暴的光
磨快尖利的鸟嘴　知道啄哪儿更为致命
啄她　碎肉零落　枝头震荡

一双第一天已深深看进肉里的眼睛
用必死的诗意　让你想像一次猛烈的活
带着孤零零悬挂的被引爆的表情

you take all year to imagine inserting the kernel stuck inside you
a revolving axle   a kind of force you want to deny
can't deny   autumn is a slow fire for death and hanging too

indigo logic that lifts you swaying in space
metres above the ground   when flushed fruits hold their kernels and rub
wind touches you   whoever wants to can touch you in this place

cold nails your inner being   sweet limitless only then for yourself
rot has a handle   clutching and smelling the fishy fragrance of sex
on a golden barb you hang yourself

metres above the world   given over to the crudest brilliance
beak that sharpens its point   knows where pecking is more mortal
pecks her   broken flesh withered   vibrating branch

two eyes that saw deep into the flesh on that first day
take the poetic of necessary death   to make you imagine one fierce life
a detonated facial expression hanging and lonely

10．圣丁香之海

这一刻无限大　花　迸开在人的尽头
激动中　天空的紫色　海的白色
驶出我们身上每处奋张的港口

水里满是心跳　水的厄运是一生去触摸
一根埋在肉中绷直抽动的管子
一个不停拧紧蓓蕾乳头的四月

输送　灿烂皮肤下我们的无知
紫色和白色　都被体内的黑暗驱赶到空中
漫无目的　以急急奔赴一次自焚为目的

这一刻　碎裂的生殖器鲜艳就是目送
春天的香味就象烟味　一把把绸伞撑开
末日抵进嘴里　惊叫都学着鸟鸣

肉体的形象是不够的　最终需要一滴泪
出走到花园里　星际嫩嫩漂流
每阵风吹走大海

this instant is infinitely large   flowers   spurt at humans' end
in excitation   purple of the sky white of the sea
drive out of the harbours on our flesh forced and opened

water is full of heartbeats   water's bad luck is life-long touch
the stiff twitching tube buried in the flesh
April endlessly twisting nipple buds in its clutch

shipped   our ignorance beneath splendid skin
purple and white   expelled into the sky by the body's own dark
random   aiming for the hasty rush to self-immolation

this instant   the shine of shattered sex organs is a long look of goodbye
spring's perfume like smoke's smell   silken parasols opening one by one
final day lowered into our mouth   all your cries learning from a bird's cry

only the body's image isn't enough   at last a tear drop has fallen
leaving for the garden   stars tenderly drifting
each breath of wind blowing away the ocean

Printed in the United Kingdom
by Lightning Source UK Ltd.
118137UK00002B/178-195